Original title:
The Sweetest Orchard

Copyright © 2025 Creative Arts Management OÜ
All rights reserved.

Author: Riley Donovan
ISBN HARDBACK: 978-1-80586-432-5
ISBN PAPERBACK: 978-1-80586-904-7

Aromatic Reverie

In a land where fruits do dance,
Lemons joke with a merry glance.
Cherries giggle, oh what a spree,
Their pits are the punchlines, can't you see?

Bananas slip with quite a flair,
Peaches blush, light as air.
Limes are sour, but don't you pout,
They're the wisecrackers hanging out!

Orchard of Sundrenched Joy

Nestled 'neath a sunny beam,
Apples scheme, they plot and dream.
Grapes wear sunglasses, looking fine,
They sip on juice, it's party time!

Pears do pirouettes, oh so spry,
While plums are texting, "Wait, oh my!"
A fruit parade, with laughter loud,
The blooms are cheering, "Aren't we proud?"

Blossom Kisses

In the orchard, flowers play,
Swaying gently, come what may.
Daisies whisper, tulips tease,
Buzzing bees just want some cheese!

Roses giggle, sharing glee,
"I'll steal the show!" says the bumblebee.
Daffodils don their jester hats,
They prank the squirrels and laugh with cats!

Essence of Eden

Here the cherries throw a bash,
While coconuts engage in splash.
Radishing roots dig in the ground,
Their dance-off leaves folks spellbound!

Mangoes wear their finest zest,
On tippy toes, they try their best.
With laughter blossoming all around,
This happy place knows joy unbound!

Orchard's Secret Serenade

In a grove where apples grin,
Cherries giggle, where do we begin?
Fruits wear hats, it's quite a scene,
Lemons dance to the tunes unseen.

Peaches blush in the summer sun,
While plums chuckle, oh what fun!
Grapes gossip on a leafy vine,
Whispering secrets of the divine.

Lush Canopy of Delight

Beneath the branches, squirrels conspire,
Dropping acorns, raising the choir.
Dancing leaves in the golden light,
Nature's mishaps, oh what a sight!

Bananas slip in a playful chase,
Oranges giggle, oh, what a race!
A coconut drops with a thud and a splash,
All in laughter, they make a bash.

Serenade of Succulent Spheres

In juicy realms where berries play,
Funny figures frolic all day.
Pineapples wear their spiky crowns,
While mangoes wear the juiciest frowns.

Strawberries whisper silly dreams,
Raspberries giggle, bursting at seams.
Under the sun, they throw a ball,
Harvesting laughs, the sweetest of all.

Tender Roots in Sunlight

Roots are poking out just for fun,
Tickling feet under the sun.
Carrots laugh in the garden plot,
While radishes wave, giving a shot.

Tomatoes blush, they just can't hide,
Turning red with a wink and a stride.
Potatoes roll, having a spree,
In this patch, all is whimsy and glee.

Apple Blossoms and Honeyed Skies

In a land where apples sway,
The bees buzzed in a silly play,
One bee said, 'I'll take the lead!'
While tripping over every seed!

The flowers giggled, bright and bold,
Sharing whispers, tales retold,
A squirrel danced in a froggy suit,
While ants were marching, oh so cute!

Sweet Harvest Melodies

Grapes were strumming on their vines,
Singing songs with cheeky lines,
Berries joined with jazzy flair,
Wiggly worms began to pair!

A pumpkin played the tambourine,
The carrots pranced in shades of green,
Gathering friends for a harvest show,
With laughter that would steal the show!

Enchanted Grove Secrets

The trees whispered, 'Can you hear?'
A raccoon said, 'Don't come too near!'
He wore a cloak of leafy fright,
Claiming to be the king of night!

But when he tripped on his own tail,
The forest roared with a loud wail,
'Oh, Raccoon, you've lost your crown!'
And everyone laughed in the round!

Rays of Ripe Promise

The sunbeams danced on golden bread,
While veggies wore hats upon their heads,
'Lettuce feast!' they sang with glee,
As carrots skated by the brie!

A mischief-maker, a cheeky pear,
Juggled fruits with a humorous flair,
Tumbling down amid the cheer,
Yelling, 'Catch me, I'm over here!'

Rustic Serenades

In the grove where apples dance,
The squirrels hold a froggy prance.
With peaches wearing silly hats,
And grapes that joke with silly chats.

A plum fell down with quite a thud,
While cherries giggled in a flood.
The farmer laughed, he lost his shoe,
As berries played tag, oh how they grew!

The pears plotted mischief, oh so grand,
While raspberries formed a band unplanned.
With every stomp, the juices spilled,
And all at once, the orchard thrilled.

So gather round, it's a fruit affair,
Where laughter blooms and fills the air.
Each bite's a chuckle, sweet delight,
In nature's jest, the world feels right.

Secrets among the Boughs

Beneath the leaves, old tales abound,
Of sneaky seeds that dance around.
The green beans whisper secrets low,
While carrots plot their next big show.

A melon claimed the crown today,
While others giggled, lost in play.
The tomatoes threw a splashy ball,
And cucumbers rolled, not shy at all.

The corn stalks leaned in, quite bemused,
As radishes felt overly used.
With every rustle, laughter grew,
In nature's game of peekaboo.

So climb the trees, embrace the fun,
Where every fruit is never done.
Among the boughs, a joy to glean,
The garden's quirks, a wondrous scene.

Vibrations of Verdant Beauty

In the meadow, bugs perform ballet,
While daisies host a cheeky soiree.
The sunbeams tap, a rhythm bright,
And butterflies join in the flight.

Ripe tomatoes roll with flair so bold,
While peas tell tales of days of old.
The carrots wouldn't be outdone,
In their green tops, all in fun!

With leafy friends, the rhythm sways,
As fruits and veggies dance and play.
The melody of sweet delight,
In every crunch, the joy ignites.

So sway, oh orchard, sing your tunes,
Beneath the laughter of the moons.
Each harvest brings a hearty grin,
In nature's dance, we all join in.

Blossom-laden Dreams

In a garden of giggles, the fruits do sway,
An apple in a hat, it wants to play.
A pear with a mustache starts to dance,
While grapes in a row do the grapevine prance.

Cherries in sunglasses, feeling quite cool,
Watermelons splashing, oh, what a pool!
Kiwi cracking jokes, making everyone roar,
In this fruity circus, who could ask for more?

Beneath the Shade of Kindness

Under trees of laughter, we lay down our heads,
With peaches as pillows, and warmth in our spreads.
A banana in flip-flops is telling a tale,
While oranges roll by in a cozy sail.

The lemon's quite sour, but tells the best jokes,
Cucumbers are giggling, in their leafy cloaks.
Juicy friendships blossom by sunshine's embrace,
In this fruity laughter, we all find our place.

Fruits of the Heart

Berries in a basket, plotting a scheme,
To throw a grand party, oh, what a dream!
A fig with a feather, a prune in a suit,
Bananas rehearse, for their dance to salute.

Peach cobbler's the DJ, spinning tunes from the past,
At this festival of flavor, friendship's unsurpassed.
With laughter as confetti, let the good times roll,
In this fruity fiesta, we nourish the soul.

Tasting the Sun

With strawberries sipping on lemonade chill,
Pineapples' laughter gives everyone a thrill.
Coconuts giggle, 'We're the nutty crew!'
As they roll down the hill, yell, 'Woo-hoo, woo-hoo!'

Tropical fun as we dance in delight,
Mangoes and melons, all shining so bright.
Under skies sprinkled with zesty good cheer,
We feast on the joy, for the harvest is near.

The Enchanted Grove's Lullaby

In a grove where giggles grow,
Fruits wear hats, putting on a show.
The apples dance, the pears all sing,
Even the lemons do their thing.

A squirrel juggles nuts so bold,
While a bear tries to do what he's told.
With every laugh and silly sound,
Joy and chaos can be found.

Sunshine winks through leafy trees,
A breeze that brings both laughs and sneeze.
Come join the fun, don't be late,
This grove is truly first-rate!

Echoes of Nature's Abundance

In the orchard, where laughter flies,
Baving berries wear funny ties.
They gossip low, but oh so sweet,
Talking tales about their feet.

A pear once slipped, a silly sight,
And rolled away, oh what a fright!
But all the fruits just laughed out loud,
A fruity prank that drew a crowd.

The breeze carries giggles near,
As cherries joke, "We've got no fear!"
Comical moments fill the air,
In this land of fruity flair.

Beneath the Boughs of Promise

Beneath the branches, high and low,
An orange claims, "I'm quite the show!"
"I'm juicy, bright, can make you smile,"
While lemons pout, "We're in denial!"

A cherry tried to climb a tree,
But instead got stuck—oh woe is he!
The laughter echoes, round they go,
With every joke, their spirits glow.

The vines are filled with silly tunes,
Bananas dance under a pair of moons.
In this realm of fruity delight,
Silly moments shine so bright.

Flavorful Fantasies in Bloom

In a land where flavors burst and play,
Strawberries dream of a funny ballet.
They twirl and spin on evening leaves,
While giggling grapes drop funny thieves.

A pumpkin once wore a funny hat,
Declaring loudly, "I'm the boss of that!"
While turnips snicker, hiding behind,
This garden's humor is intertwined.

Jokester fruits in colors so bold,
Tell tales of antics that never get old.
Come reap the laughs, they bloom in glee,
A whimsical feast, just wait and see!

Fragrant Trails of Juicy Memories

In the twilight glow they prance,
With berry hats we do our dance.
Tangerines roll down the lane,
Laughing at the sun's last grain.

Bouncing on cherries, giggles spurt,
Banana peels—who's wearing dirt?
Grapes slip by with a squeaky cheer,
As fruit flies buzz, let's make it clear!

Dance of the Fruit-laden Breeze

A peach parade on the green grass,
With watermelon smiles, let's make it last!
Pineapple hats, oh what a sight,
We whirl and twirl, a fruity delight.

Mango spins, in the warm night air,
Laughing blueberries everywhere!
Lemons throw shade, but we don't mind,
In this fruit fiesta, joy's blind.

Harvest Moonlit Revelry

Underneath the moon's soft glow,
We munch on fruit as stars throw.
A rambunctious grape climbs a tree,
While others giggle with jubilee.

The apples sing a merry tune,
While oranges bop to a silly swoon.
Tarts and pies in a goofy heap,
Dreams of flavors that run deep.

Canvas of Petals and Juices

In sticky hands, we paint the ground,
With raspberry splashes all around.
Cotton candy clouds drift on by,
As kiwi birds begin to fly.

Sours and sweets in a playful brawl,
Dancing through this fruity hall.
We giggle at the fruit parade,
As cherries wink, unafraid.

Cherries in a Sunbeam

In a garden bright and bold,
Cherries giggle, tales unfold.
They wear little hats of red,
Making mischief where they tread.

Sunshine sprinkles laughter loud,
While bees dance, just so proud.
Every twist, a fruity prank,
A cherry jester on the plank.

Tapestry of Tenderness

Little fruits weave tales so fine,
Bananas slip on jokes divine.
Grapes gather round to share a laugh,
In this fruity, happy staff.

Apples bob in playful cheer,
Chasing pears that scurry near.
Every hug's a fruity game,
In a land where fun's the aim.

Juicy Tales Under Starlit Skies

Under the stars, oranges sing,
Tickling the night with their zing.
Lemons laugh with pucker smiles,
As they dance through leafy aisles.

Blueberries burst with glee and dare,
To spin around on midnight air.
With every squish, a story told,
Of friendships juicy, brave, and bold.

Petal Rain

When petals fall, they play their tricks,
Dancing on dips, they twist and flick.
The flowers laugh, the wind agrees,
Turning gardens into comedies.

Tulips paint the skies with cheer,
Twirling soft, they persevere.
Every petal tells a tale,
Of whimsy, joy, and happy mail.

The Orchard's Timeless Embrace

Bouncing apples on the ground,
They giggle with each thud and sound.
A pear doing a little dance,
Trying hard to catch a glance.

Cherries wearing silly hats,
Dancing with the bouncing bats.
A prune that thought it was a peach,
Claimed a crown, but it's out of reach.

Oranges spinning round with glee,
Call it fruit-a-laughter spree.
Bananas slip and have a laugh,
While figs take selfies on their path.

In this grove, the humor grows,
With sweet surprises in each dose.
So come and join this fruity scheme,
Where laughter's more than just a dream.

Harvesting the Essence of Joy

Gathering fruits with giggling joy,
Plums wear socks, a playful ploy.
Watermelons rolling down the lane,
Making a splash, oh what a gain!

Strawberries start a tickle fight,
Raspberries insist they own the night.
Peaches sing in harmonized tunes,
Sending giggles to the moon.

Lemons dressed in sunny cheer,
Juggling limes that bounce and veer.
Cantaloupes make marshmallow pies,
While dreaming of sweet, sugary skies.

Join us here, in bright delight,
Among these fruits, everything's right.
Laugh away the garden's charm,
In joy, they gather, safe from harm.

Fruitful Whispers

Whispers float from branch to branch,
Grapes gossip, plotting a prance.
A kiwi winks with a silly grin,
While bananas trade their peel for skin.

Mulberries blend in a swirling groove,
With apricots trying to bust a move.
Pineapples wear sunglasses tight,
While coconuts revel in delight.

Fruits telling pun-laden jokes,
Even the roots shake, they're no hoax.
"Orange you glad we're having fun?"
Said the apples, "Oh, we've just begun!"

So gather 'round, let's spread the cheer,
In fruity whispers, laughter's near.
Take a bite of joy and bliss,
In this orchard, you can't miss!

Boughs of Bliss

Boughs dangle heavy with ripe surprise,
Cherries laughing under sunny skies.
Apples tell tales of their grassy dreams,
While lemons plot outrageous schemes.

Peaches giggle in a sunlit hug,
Hiding secrets like a cozy bug.
Pears play catch, oh what a scene,
While plums become the fruit queen bee.

Happiness rustles in every leaf,
Crafting laughter, beyond belief.
Coconuts float in silly skits,
As oranges get tangled in their wits.

So step on in, where joy unfolds,
Amidst sweet fruits and tales retold.
Here in the boughs, laughter's free,
Come taste the fun, come share with me!

Taste of Sunlit Dreams

In a grove where giggles grow,
Lemons dance in rows that glow.
Apples whisper cheeky remarks,
While cherries organize their larks.

A peach in a tutu twirls with flair,
Bananas bounce without a care.
Kiwis chuckle, telling tales,
While plums plot treasure map trails.

Mangoes munch on candy trees,
Sharing secrets with buzzing bees.
Grapes wear hats, all tight and neat,
Inviting everyone for a treat.

As laughter drips from branch to ground,
Fruit confetti rains all around.
In this orchard, joy's the scheme,
Sweet is the taste of sunlit dreams.

Currents of Honeyed Air

In a field where laughter flows,
Bumblebees wear tiny clothes.
Roses blush with laughter's sound,
Waltzing freely, spinning round.

A pumpkin juggles, quite the sight,
Carrots wiggle, feeling bright.
Spinach flexes, knows it's strong,
Swapping jokes just all day long.

Tomatoes giggle, red with glee,
While corn plays hide and seek with me.
In this breeze where fun takes flight,
Honey drips under warm sunlight.

Peas in pods share gossip sweet,
Nature's own hilarious meet.
Here in air where spirits soar,
Life's a dance, forevermore.

The Abundant Tapestry of Life

In a patchwork of squash so bright,
Zucchini wears a polka-dot night.
Cabbages gossip, leek's in on it,
While peppers throw a colorful fit.

Radishes roll with a cheeky grin,
As cabernet grapes dare to spin.
Cucumbers join in, all slim and spry,
And artichokes giggle, oh my, oh my!

Corncobs wear monocles, it seems,
While avocados spread their dreams.
This garden, a fiesta of mirth,
Each sprout sings loudly of its worth.

With roots that twist and branches that sway,
Life's a carnival, come what may.
In every seed, a punchline's rife,
In this grand tapestry of life.

Radiance Among Twining Vines

Lively tendrils stretch and twine,
As laughter curls around the vine.
Cucumbers giggle, seeking sun,
While squash competes in a spirited run.

Grapevines weave stories with flair,
Each cluster shares a juicy dare.
Bees chatter about their busy flight,
While radishes blush, feeling quite light.

Tomatoes boast of their bright tint,
In sun-drenched glory, there's no hint.
Cantaloupes don hats, big and round,
In this patch, silly joys abound.

Among the vines, vibrant and free,
Nature's jesters playfully agree.
Through this clever dance and rhyme,
Radiance sparkles, one laugh at a time.

Nectar's Embrace

In the garden where the bees joke,
A squirrel wears a tiny cloak.
Honey drips from every tree,
Even plants hum in glee.

A peach is dancing with a pear,
While cherries play in the warm air.
Lemons giggle, oranges chuckle,
Bouncing round like kids in a huddle.

The mulberries tell tales of pride,
Each berry on a juicy ride.
With every bite, a laugh erupts,
As laughter from the fruit erupts.

So join the party, take a slice,
In this orchard, nothing's precise.
With nature's tricks, we won't complain,
Just taste the joy and feel the gain.

Harvest Moon Serenade

Under the glow of a bright moon,
The apples sing a merry tune.
A cantaloupe strums on a vine,
While grapes sip juice and feel divine.

Pumpkins wear hats and dance in rows,
While broccoli flaunts its green clothes.
The carrots join in, with wiggly feet,
As vegetables sway to the beat.

Stars twinkle above, play peek-a-boo,
As the veggies share secrets, just a few.
Whispers of laughter fill the night,
In this garden, all feels just right.

So, laugh along with the harvest cheer,
Grab a friend, bring some cheer.
In this moonlit orchard, spirits ignite,
With every giggle, the world feels bright.

Garden of Golden Delights

In a garden where no one wears shoes,
Carrots gossip about the news.
Potatoes roll and tumble along,
While radishes sing a silly song.

Peas play hide and seek in the grass,
While onions tease and make a sass.
Tomatoes blush, but don't hide too long,
They love the fun and join in the throng.

Sunflowers wobble, a dancing crew,
With giggles that sprout from morning dew.
A parade of veggies, oh what a sight,
In this patch of fun, everything's right.

Come join the fun, leave worries behind,
In this garden, humor's unconfined.
With every bite, a chuckle we share,
Delights abound, laughter in the air.

Symphony of Ripened Dreams

The berries play their sweetest chords,
While cucumbers strum with green swords.
As peaches spin across the ground,
In this melodic world, joy is found.

Watermelons burst out in song,
Making every critter sing along.
With ripe bananas dancing with flair,
Laughter echoes, spreading everywhere.

A zucchini plays the drums so loud,
While bell peppers lead a jolly crowd.
The fruit parade marches with glee,
A symphony of flavors, wild and free.

So lend an ear to this fruity dream,
Where laughter flows, and joy's the theme.
Take a bite, let the flavor beam,
In this orchestra, life's a gleam.

Whispers of Fruity Bliss

In a land where apples giggle,
Pears wear hats that make them wiggle.
Bananas slip on peels so bright,
While grapes dance in the moonlight.

Cherries gossip in their trees,
Sharing secrets on the breeze.
Plums in pajamas, oh what a sight,
While lemons laugh with all their might.

Peaches throw a party, oh so grand,
Mangoes play drums with a fruity band.
Everyone's invited, come take a spin,
A fruity fiesta that's sure to win!

So come join the fun, don't be shy,
Fruitful antics will surely fly.
With every bite, a joke retold,
A sweet, juicy world that's pure gold.

Golden Harvest Dreams

In a field of dreams where cornflakes grow,
Strawberries play hide and seek, oh no!
Kiwis in capes, saving the day,
With each crunchy bite, they fly away.

Carrots wear glasses, reading the news,
While radishes sport their very best shoes.
Spinach does yoga, trying to zen,
"Breathe deeply now, let's do it again!"

A pumpkin rolls in, filled with cheer,
Wearing a hat, it's the best time of year.
Tomatoes stand proudly in their red suits,
Throwing a bash, with all the roots!

So come take a stroll beneath the sun,
In a garden where laughter's never done.
In fields of gold, where fun will scheme,
Life's just a bowl of cereal dream!

Nectar-Kissed Blossoms

In a garden where bees wear tiny hats,
Flowers converse with chubby cats.
Buttercups chuckle, showing their glee,
While daisies twirl like they're on spree!

Sweet nectar dripping, making bees buzz,
Roses play bingo, just because.
Tulips gossip about who wears best,
In bloom-style fashion, they're quite obsessed.

Bumblebees tumble, falling in laughter,
Over butterfly secrets and what comes after.
Violets in tutus, spinning around,
In a world so silly, joy can be found!

So dance with the daisies, swirl with delight,
In nectar-kissed moments, the world feels bright.
When flowers are funny, and humor is free,
Join the riot where laughter grows like a tree.

Symphony of Ripening Boughs

Underneath the apple tree, oh what a sight,
Chickens are waltzing, oh what a flight!
Peaches play flute, while bananas sing,
In the jammed-up orchards, joy's the real king.

Grapes are gossiping, hanging around,
As squirrels orchestrate a nutty sound.
Oranges breakdance, citrusy and bright,
With lemons conducting the band at night.

In this fruity symphony, laughter's the score,
Every branch sways, wanting more and more.
Nature's amusing, in its own way,
Let's join the concert, come out and play!

So grab a fruit, let's get the groove,
In the symphony of trees, we'll bust a move.
With melodies sweet and rhymes that tease,
Together we'll create the perfect breeze.

Floral Crescendo in Full Bloom

In a field where colors clash,
Petals wear their brightest sash.
Bees in tuxedos buzz around,
Dancing with a silly bound.

Sunflowers act like they're on stage,
Hamming it up, but we just gauge.
Tulips giggle, swaying low,
Making tulip tales to bestow.

Daisies laughing, in a row,
Claim they've got the best lawn show.
Pansies wink, they're not so meek,
Joining in the funny streak.

With vines that twist and leaves that prance,
Nature throws a grand old dance.
Laughter blooms with every sound,
In this botanical playground!

Under the Canvas of Green Canopies

Beneath the shades of leafy sprees,
Lizards chatter, buzzing bees.
Squirrels wear their spiky hats,
Swinging light like acrobats.

A rabbit slips, and what a sight!
Springing back with all its might.
Frogs leap in a merry choir,
Belting tunes that set hearts on fire.

Branches sway and sometimes creak,
While birds gossip, cheek to cheek.
The woodland critters in a game,
Chasing shadows, oh what a fame!

With roots that twist and saplings spry,
Nature laughs with a winked eye.
Underneath this leafy dome,
You'll find laughter finds its home!

Blossom's Gentle Farewell

As petals drift like sunny dreams,
The breeze giggles, or so it seems.
Blossoms wave their last goodbye,
Saying, "Don't be sad, oh my!"

Fluffy clouds play hide and seek,
While flowers show their cheeky streak.
"Count our colors, one, two, three!"
Each petal whispers, "Look at me!"

A gust runs by, they swirl and twirl,
Creating chaos in a whirl.
Nature plays its funny tricks,
Farewell blooms, give cheeky kicks!

As the season takes a bow,
The garden giggles, "Don't you cow!
We'll come again, just take a seat,
For nature's humor can't be beat!"

Sweet Drops of Nature's Bounty

Under trees, the fruits do hang,
Every berry sings and sang.
Pineapples wear their spiky crown,
As bananas slip, then tumble down.

Cherries blushing, holding tight,
Grapes giggling, what a sight!
Watermelons in a spree,
Spilling juice that's free for me!

Apples gossip, sweet and tart,
While oranges play the juicy part.
In this feast, there's no complaint,
Except from pears who faint and paint.

But as the party rolls along,
Nature hums its merry song.
With every drop a sugary cheer,
In the orchard, laughter's near!

Pudding Twirls and Tart Confections

In a land where fruits play chess,
Pudding twirls in a fruity dress.
Tarts with giggles, pies that grin,
Berry jests as laughter spins.

A lemon joked, it made a jest,
While cherries danced, they did their best.
Whipped cream swirled in a happy spin,
Sweet tooth buddy, let the feast begin!

Grapes are rolling, what a sight,
Making wine in pure delight.
And every fruit is in on fun,
Join the party, end the pun!

So grab a spoon, a fork, or a slice,
Cherries just slipped on some ice!
With every bite, we cheer and shout,
In this circus, there's no doubt!

Elysian Orchard Echoes

In a grove where laughter grows,
Fragrant blooms with silly shows.
Bananas slip and oranges slide,
Ticklish apples take a ride.

A pear declared, 'I'm quite the catch!'
While others giggled, 'We'll attach!'
Pear-fect puns, it's all in play,
Fruitful jokes brighten the day.

Nuts perform in fancy hats,
While berries tease with silly spats.
Grapefruit winks, a cheeky tease,
While all the fruits join in with ease.

Join the fun in this orchard fair,
Forget your worries, shed your care!
With every laugh, the trees will sway,
Echoing joy in bright array!

Harmony of Harvest

In orchards full of glee and cheer,
Tomatoes juggle, aren't they dear?
Cucumbers leap, toss pies with flair,
Every harvest sings with care.

A pumpkin tried to be a star,
But got stuck, a funny tar.
Tripped on peas, gave quite a show,
Come see the crops, oh what a row!

Raspberries whisper, 'Let's all dance,'
While radishes twirl in a trance.
With every crunch and sprinkle bright,
The laughter echoes through the night.

So gather 'round, both big and small,
In this patch, there's joy for all!
For in this harvest's merry tune,
Laughter blossoms, night or noon!

Reflections of a Fruitful Realm

In a realm of fruits, all round and bright,
Pickles wearing hats, what a sight!
Watermelons dance, making friends,
While berry bands play tunes that blend.

Peaches giggle, share their dreams,
While plums burst forth with silly schemes.
Lemonade rivers flow with cheer,
Sipping joy, bring laughter near!

Strawberries sing in red and green,
A fruit fiesta, oh what a scene!
Bananas slip, but never fall,
As joy and puns unite us all.

So let us roam this fruitful land,
With every giggle, hand in hand.
In this sweet realm, where laughter seems,
The fruit of fun fulfills our dreams!

The Taste of Sunshine

In a garden where laughter blooms,
Sunlight plays, dispelling glooms.
Bees wear hats, the ants parade,
Dancing fruit, the jokes they made.

Oranges juggle in the breeze,
Cherries giggle among the trees.
Bananas slip with a banana peel,
Even the apples like to squeal.

Lemons burst with sour delight,
As melons roll out of sheer fright.
Peaches wear their fluff with pride,
All together, they decided!

So when you bite, expect a grin,
For in this patch, we all win.
Every fruit drops a funny pun,
The taste of sunshine, oh what fun!

Fragrant Floral Ballads

Petals dance in a breeze of cheer,
Roses wink, "We're glad you're here!"
Daisies giggle tucked in a patch,
"Hurry up, you're missing the match!"

Lilies sing in brilliant hues,
Composing songs with fragrant views.
Tulips twirl in fancy dress,
Each one trying to impress!

Bumblebees hum a buzzing tune,
Whispering secrets under the moon.
"Oh, snap!" said the daffodil bright,
"Did you hear that joke last night?"

Amongst the laughter, scents collide,
In this garden, humor won't hide.
Fragrant notes in every line,
Blooming joy, oh how divine!

Serenade of Seasoned Trees

Oaks are wise with ancient laughs,
Their branches scratching silly drafts.
Pines stick to their pointy game,
Dropping needles, oh what a shame!

Willows swish with grace and flair,
"Come join the dance, if you dare!"
Seasons change, they can't resist,
Swaying together, a leafy twist.

Maple plays the sweet old song,
"Dance with me, you can't go wrong!"
Cypress spins with all its might,
Tripping happily, pure delight.

So when you walk on this earth,
Join the trees for all they're worth.
In their shade, humor grows tall,
Laugh with them, let's have a ball!

Orchard Dreams

In a land where fruits wear hats,
Laughter sprouts among the brats.
Plum parades on a sunny day,
"Marco!" calls out the pears at play.

Peppers joke in colors bright,
Laughing hard, what a sight!
Tomatoes blush with every tease,
Saying, "Oh, will you please?"

Berries mingle in a foot race,
"Can you keep up? Show us your pace!"
Pineapples cheer from the stands,
Shouting loudly, cheering bands.

So gather round, let's make a wish,
In this orchard, every fruit's delish.
Dreams of fun dance on each branch,
Join the frolic, take a chance!

Blossoms Swaying in the Breeze

In a garden filled with blooms,
A bumblebee dusts off his plumes.
He thinks he's quite the suave champ,
Buzzing around like he's at a stamp.

Petals giggle in soft delight,
As squirrels plan a nutty flight.
A butterfly flaunts with great flair,
While the garden gnomes just stare.

The Alchemy of Aromas

The scent of flowers fills the air,
But the gardener's socks? A nightmare!
With every step, the blooms do wilt,
As he tips over, nearly spilt.

The daisies chuckle, the roses blush,
A cat leaps up, causing a rush.
'Was that a mouse?' the daisies sigh,
While the gardener wonders, 'Why oh why?'

In the Arms of Nature

A little plant tries to find its place,
But keeps getting lost in a flower's lace.
It asks a leaf for tips and tricks,
Who just replies, 'Learn some good kicks!'

The oak tree laughs, so strong and bold,
While telling tales that never get old.
A rabbit hops in with a munch,
As the garden laughs at their silly brunch.

Heartbeats in the Garden

The sun pokes out with a golden grin,
Encouraging the veggies to begin.
But carrots dance like they're on a spree,
While the onions cry out, 'Let us be free!'

A tomato rolls, thinking it can race,
Tripping over its own base.
As peas snicker and join the fun,
In the garden, laughter has just begun.

A Symphony of Colorful Cravings

In the garden of giggles, fruits take a bow,
Peaches wearing sunglasses, oh look at them now!
Bananas are dancing, what a wild scene,
Cherries on top cheer, it's a fruity routine!

With lemons that chuckle and limes that roll,
Each berry's a joker, they play their own role.
Grapes in a conga, oh what a sight,
Fruit salad's a party that's pure delight!

But watch out for pears with their sly little grins,
They'll tease you for chuckles and win with their spins.
In this colorful circus, the laughter just flows,
Join in the fun, where the fruit always glows!

Under the sky where humor is ripe,
Every bite's a punchline, each taste full of hype.
So bring on the laughter, the sweetness, the cheer,
In this fruity delight, there's joy to spare here!

Whimsical Orchard Tales

Once in a grove where giggles reside,
A cornucopia of laughter, it's quite a ride!
Apples wear hats, talking loud with delight,
While walnuts tell jokes in the dark of the night.

Strawberries frolic in polka-dot shoes,
While cantaloupes share their most colorful views.
The peaches hold court with their fuzzy great flair,
Making fun of the apples, what a juicy affair!

The figs tell tall tales of winding vine paths,
While pears roll their eyes at the old "how he laughs."
Cherries sit on thrones made of green leafy crowns,
As they play king and queen without any frowns!

So gather your friends and come share in the fun,
In this quirky orchard, there's laughter for everyone!
With fruits that are silly, their jesting profound,
Each tale more amusing, where joy can be found!

Beneath the Canopy of Abundance

Beneath the branches where silliness grows,
Coconuts giggle and giddy mangoes pose.
A pear in a bowtie serves punch with a grin,
While strawberries tease, let the hilarity begin!

Oranges are juggling, their zest on display,
While limes roll about, laughing all the way.
The cherries pull pranks, oh what a bunch,
Creating a fruit bowl that's ready for lunch!

The grapes tie their shoes for a fancy parade,
With fruit flies as music, it'll never fade.
Tomatoes wear masquerades, green ones in queues,
In this harvest of laughter, they'll spread all the news!

A red apple whispers, "They're ripe for some cheer,"
As peaches agree they're the fruit of the year.
So join in the fun where laughter is grand,
In this bounteous bower, it's joy—understand?

Harvesting Dreams

In a patch full of giggles where dreams sprout like seeds,
Pineapples bloom visions and dance to our needs.
Fruits gather round with a whimsical glee,
To harvest the smiles that blossom for free!

The grapes sing a tune of a bouncy delight,
While peaches throw parties beneath the moonlight.
Bananas swap tales of their trips down the groove,
In a harvest of laughter, we all find our move!

Cherries don crowns of the craziest styles,
With plums in disguise, cracking jokes with big smiles.
The laughter flows freely in this quirky domain,
As we all join the feast, let's dance in the rain!

So pick up your basket; come gather your dreams,
In this orchard of humor, nothing's as it seems.
Every bite tells a story, each taste is supreme,
With fun in abundance, we're "harvesting" dreams!

Ripened Secrets

In a grove where fruits align,
Lemons giggle, and apples whine.
Bananas brag of their great peel,
While cherries laugh as they steal a meal.

Pears whisper tales of a juicy past,
As playful seeds scatter so fast.
Every fruit claims it's the best,
But they all know it's just a jest.

Under thickets, they form a band,
Conducting choirs of the land.
With each pluck, secrets take flight,
And every harvest brings pure delight.

So join the fun in this ripe show,
Where every bite's an amusing go.
In the laughter, the flavors blend,
In our fruity world, there's no end!

A Tangle of Ripe Memories

There's a vine that sings and twirls,
With berries dancing, flashing curls.
Old squashes tell tales, puffing out,
While peas roll their eyes, getting stout.

A cantaloupe chuckles at its size,
While kiwi jokes about disguise.
Tomatoes tease with their red hue,
As cucumbers ponder what to do.

Grapes hang low, sharing sly glee,
And radishes hope for more esprit.
In this patch, humor's the key,
Entwined in memories, wild and free.

So let's gather, make a toast,
To the funny fruits we love the most!
For in this tangle, laughter's ripe,
With every bite, we're the hype!

Savoring Sweetness

Peaches blush with a cheeky grin,
While plums boast of their thick skin.
Oranges squirt a citrus joke,
And raspberries start to choke.

Pineapples wear crowns, strutting their stuff,
While pomegranates think they're tough.
No fruit's shy as they all parade,
In this fruity, funny escapade.

With each crunch, the laughter breaks,
As jellybeans taste-test your fakes.
Fruit salads dressed in giggly cheer,
Layered sweetness, drawing near.

So let's snack on this tasty crew,
In a festival of flavors true!
Savoring sweetness, with glee we shout,
In this orchard, there's no doubt!

Beneath the Canopy of Whimsy

Beneath branches where pranks unfold,
Nutty squirrels throw down bold!
With acorns bouncing off their heads,
While fruits giggle in their beds.

A merry breeze whispers, 'Play fair!'
But the oranges toss back their flair.
And fuzzy kiwis, with a wink,
Join the fray, and we all sink!

The trees shake as laughter flows,
Banquet bites mixed with rose prose.
In this magical orchard's glow,
We savor every pun and show.

So gather close, let the fun ignite,
Beneath this whimsy, pure delight!
With every giggle, the fruits rejoice,
In sweet harmony, we find our voice!

Laughter in the Orchard

Under the trees with fruits so bright,
We danced and twirled, what a delight!
But slippery ground made my friend slip,
Fell right into a basket, what a trip!

The bees buzzed loud, trying to join,
Laughing at us, oh how they did groin!
We picked juicy berries, each one a tease,
While dodging the bees with hilarious ease!

In the shade we munched, shade of the sun,
Each bite was laughter, oh what fun!
With whipped cream fingers and fruit in our hair,
Life's too sweet, beyond compare!

So here's to laughter amidst the trees,
A fruitful day with the funniest bees!
We'll laugh and dance till the day is done,
In this orchard of joy, there's always fun!

Echoes of Ripe Nostalgia

Beneath the boughs where fruits of yore,
I heard old memories whisper and roar.
A pear that winked, a plum that grinned,
A dance of laughter, where joy won't end!

We climbed up high, thinking we're wise,
Till a branch broke, oh what a surprise!
Tumbling to ground in a fruit-filled heap,
With giggles and snorts, we lay half asleep.

Old Mr. Fig, with tales to tell,
Spilled secrets of fruit, oh he knew them well.
His juicy stories made us all sigh,
While he nibbled figs, all smug and spry.

As shadows grew long, we danced in delight,
Under stars twinkling, the sky so bright.
These memories linger, oh what fun,
In the echoing orchard, we're never done!

Melting Moments of Peach

Peachy keen and all aglow,
We tossed the fruits in a wild throw.
Slipped on a skin, oh what a fall,
Laughter rang out, we belly-rolled all!

Sticky fingers, a sweet delight,
Chased by ants on a lively flight.
Our laughter echoed, around we spun,
In this sticky world, we all had fun!

"Who needs a bowl?" my friend declared,
As she caught a peach, her cheeks all bared.
The juice flowed down, so wild and free,
We laughed so hard, it was pure glee!

So here's to crunches and squishy bites,
Days filled with laughter, and sweet delights.
Each melting moment, we'll treasure dear,
In this fruity paradise, we've nothing to fear!

A Dance Among the Apples

Under the apples, we spun around,
With giggles and laughter, we hit the ground.
One apple catapulted, and who knows where,
Landed right there in Grandma's hair!

We broke into fits as she looked so shocked,
With a cheeky grin, all fear we blocked.
She twirled and laughed in the orchard's spree,
"Who tossed that fruit?" oh it must be me!

In this paradise of red and green,
We danced as if we were all on the scene.
An apple a day? We had enough,
Juggling fruits in laughter, isn't that tough?

As twilight called, and stars peeked through,
Our apple dance party was far from blue.
With stories to share and laughter that sticks,
In this merry orchard, we found our kicks!

Orchard Whispers at Twilight

Under the boughs, the apples grin,
Squirrels plotting a treasure within.
A pear with a wink, a peach with a laugh,
Making mischief, their juicy craft.

Glimmers of moonlight dance on the floor,
While giggles of fruit echo more and more.
The plums tell tales of a daring heist,
As the ripened fruits share bites of the night.

A rogue rabbit hops, quite out of tune,
Singing to stars, under the moon.
The branches shake, the laughter peals,
In this fruity world, every fruit reveals.

So let's toast to the side-splitting scenes,
Where apples wear hats and dance in jeans.
In this orchard, the fun never quits,
Just watch your head! Here comes the pips!

Sunkissed Serenades

Sunshine drips from a berry's skin,
A grape with a mustache wants to win.
The bananas play tag, they twist and twirl,
While cherries giggle, trying to hurl.

A watermelon winks, rumored to sing,
As butterflies flap, trying to cling.
The peach parade marches down the lane,
With fruit florals, laughter's their refrain.

The oranges burst, their jokes so sweet,
While plum pies dance on a sticky beat.
A rumble of laughter fills the air,
In this orchard, joy's beyond compare.

So grab your pals, it's time for fun,
Where fruit-filled antics have just begun.
Each bite a giggle, each nibble a cheer,
Sunkissed adventures await us here!

Lullabies in Leafy Halls

Beneath the leaves, a lullaby hums,
Where sleepy fruits sway, while the bumblebee drums.
The apples snooze in their rosy beds,
As the mashed banana dreams in threads.

Olive branches sway with sleepy winks,
Avocado pillows, oh how it stinks!
The berries snore in a fuzzy heap,
While the fig mates chuckle, drifting to sleep.

A peach starts to giggle, dreams in the air,
While pear snorts loudly, without a care.
The night rolls in, oh so mellow tight,
In leafy halls, where laughter takes flight.

So rest your head where the fruit dreams flow,
With whispers of joy in the moon's soft glow.
These lullabies bring smiles so bright,
In our leafy sanctuary, all is delight.

Glimmers of Gold

Sunset spills over the orchard wide,
Where fruits in golden hues doth bide.
A lemon jugglers, orange shows flair,
Bananas parade, without a care.

The gold dust dances on every leaf,
While the pineapple jests, a comic chief.
With peaches that giggle and berries that spin,
Here comes the laughter, let the fun begin!

Glimmers of joy fill the evening sky,
A fruit gathering, oh my, oh my!
The sunset offers a comic feast,
In this orchard where laughter's increased.

So let the sun set on pranks and delight,
As fruits exchange jokes in the fading light.
In this playful place, with no end to the gold,
The sweetest stories of laughter unfold!

Silent Sweets of the Grove

In the shade where giggles play,
Cherries giggle, 'til they sway.
A raccoon steals a slice of pie,
While squirrels plot with a winked eye.

Lemon drops fall from high trees,
Sticky shoes dance in the breeze.
"Who spilled jam?" a crow caws loud,
As bees buzz through the happy crowd.

Beneath the whispers of the leaves,
Sweet confessions the orchard weaves.
Saplings gossip with a clap,
While fruit sneaks a midday nap.

So laugh with berries, sing with zest,
All sweet secrets, you can guess.
In this grove where fun won't stop,
We'll take a bite and laugh 'til we drop.

Petal Soft Dreams

On petals soft, the dreams parade,
Lemon-lime jigs in a fruit charade.
A bumblebee dons a tiny hat,
As donut holes roll and chat.

Peaches prank the playful bees,
Pretending to float with subtle ease.
A jester peach slips on a rind,
Spins round and round, the orchard's blind.

Sweet pies whisper silly tales,
Of dancing frogs and laughing snails.
Each fruit a clown in disguise,
Tickling fun beneath the skies.

With every chuckle, juice does flow,
As raspberry jokes steal the show.
In this dreamland, giggles gleam,
Where fruit and laughter reign supreme.

Canopy of Delights

Underneath the leafy beams,
Fruit spirits celebrate like dreams.
Bananas play tag, running fast,
Pineapples cheer, 'Eat me at last!'

A nutty squirrel in a bow tie,
Juggles acorns and shouts, "Oh my!"
Watermelons crack puns that split,
As juicy laughter makes us sit.

Orchard shadows dance all night,
While raccoons hold a fruit-themed flight.
Cider spills secrets, fizzles sound,
As a tango of flavors doth abound.

With twinkling stars and giggles sweet,
This canopy is quite the treat.
We'll vine and twine like circus clowns,
In the funnest fruit-filled town.

Juiced Memories

In a jug of memories pressed,
Lemon laughs and apple jest.
Tales of berries in a mix,
Spin funny yarns with whimsical tricks.

Tomatoes debate who wears the crown,
While strawberry jokes turn upside down.
A cantaloupe teases blender blades,
In this delirious fruit parade.

Spinach shows up in a fruit fight,
Revealing green surprises, what a sight!
Giggling lemons find ways to infuse,
Every sip, a burst of hues.

So raise your glass with a wink,
As fruity laughter makes you think:
In every drop the joy resides,
A concoction where laughter abides.

Flickering Fireflies and Fruit

In the garden, bugs held a dance,
Fruit trees swayed, taking a chance.
Fireflies flickered, wearing a glow,
Chasing the breeze on an all-you-can-eat show.

Lemons giggled, oranges played tag,
A watermelon wore a fancy swag.
Neighbors peered, with puzzled delight,
Pondering why grapes flew kites at night.

A banana slipped, threatened to fall,
While cherries gathered for a fruit ball.
Apples threw pies in a custard spree,
Who knew fruit could turn so zany and free?

With each laugh and a juicy cheer,
The night grew bright with sweet fruit beer.
So if you hear of a wacky place,
Join the fun in the orchard race!

Heartstrings in the Harvest

Midi notes played from plump pumpkins,
Each bite a musical, sweet little sums.
Harvesting laughter with every scoop,
First prize goes to the juiciest fruit troop.

The corn on the cob gave a trumpet sound,
Grapes belted tunes, all around.
Tomatoes danced with legume flair,
Who knew veggies had rhythm to share?

A scarecrow crooned in the tall stalks,
While celery swayed in quirky talks.
In the aisles of greens and golden ears,
Each note was the echo of silly cheers.

Come gather 'round, join the delight,
As joy ripens under moonlight.
In the harvest, there's music to marry,
So dance, sing, and let mischief vary!

Whispers of the Wind

Here in the garden, whispers reside,
With the fruit and the breeze, side by side.
A plum told a joke to a shy little lime,
While the apples barked in a pun-filled rhyme.

The wind giggled, swirling the leaves,
As ants wore hats, seeking reprieves.
Cucumbers chuckled at radish's wits,
Pooling their laughter with curious fits.

Pumpkins grinned, holding secrets so sweet,
While cherries debated on how to retreat.
In this land of bizarre tales untold,
The wind shared stories, both cunning and bold.

A dance in the breeze and a ripple of cheer,
As fruit trees whisper: "Come join our sphere!"
With winds that tickle and laughter that spins,
In this joyous patch, the fun never thins!

A Melodic Harvest

Nature's band, with fruits as the crew,
With trumpets of corn and a pear so true.
In this juicy fiesta, the tunes never tire,
Each berry a verse, each seed a choir.

Strawberries sang while blueberries played,
Raspberries clapped at the perfect cascade.
The almonds joined in with a quick little rap,
While peas tapped the time from a lovely nap.

The praises poured from the garden of dreams,
As melon strummed while water spilled beams.
A harvest of laughter, virtuous and spry,
Brought together by music beneath the blue sky.

So gather your friends and join in the glee,
For in this orchard, you'll dance wild and free.
With fruits as our orchestra, nature's delight,
A melodic harvest to charm the night!

www.ingramcontent.com/pod-product-compliance
Lightning Source LLC
Chambersburg PA
CBHW060138230426
43661CB00003B/476